The Dog Who Thinks He's A Fish

Acknowledgements

My thanks to the following publications where some of the poems first appeared:

Ambit, Biscuit 2002, Daily Telegraph Arvon International Poetry Competition Anthologies 2000 and *2002, Envoi, Entering the Tapestry* (Enitharmon), *Magma, Poems in the Waiting Room, Peterloo Poets Competition Anthologies 2001* and *2002, Poetry London, Smiths Knoll, Tabla, The New Writer.*

'The Dog Who Thinks He's A Fish' won first prize in the Poetry London Competition 2001. 'She' won first prize in the 1998 Tabla International Poetry Competition and 'He' won joint second prize in the 1998 Dulwich Festival Competition.

Many thanks also to Jane Anderson and Robert Seatter for helping to knock this book into shape, to Michael Laskey and the late Roy Blackman for expert encouragement, and to Jane Duran and the Thursday Group for fun and inspiration.

The Dog Who Thinks
He's A Fish

Chris Beckett

Smith/Doorstop Books

Published 2004 by
Smith/Doorstop Books
The Poetry Business
The Studio
Byram Arcade
Westgate
Huddersfield HD1 1ND

ISBN 1-902382-59-5

British Library Cataloguing-in-Publication Data. A
catalogue record for this book is available from the
British Library.

Typeset at The Poetry Business
Printed by Charlesworth, Huddersfield

Cover picture: 'Islander' by Isao Miura
Photograph by Isao Miura

Distributed by Central Books Ltd., 99 Wallis Road,
London E9 5LN

The Poetry Business gratefully acknowledges the
help of Arts Council England and Kirklees Cultural
Services.

CONTENTS

ETHIOPIA

Allumeuse

I heard the story and I thought of you –
you as a bird dodging pine trees
that hissed as the fire
tore breath from the bark,

you with wings
and a delicate beak
strafed by the shrapnel
of exploding cones,

you terrified out of your wits
and running on air
but finding the currents
suddenly savage and unpredictable,

and all the men with hoses looking up,
wondering if you'd make it,
hoping you would because
you were small and beautiful,

you almost making it
before you hit the final hoop,
emerging like a circus dog
but this time in full flame,

flapping your wings to put it out
but already too late,
fanning the flame instead,
flying on empty

for over fifty yards
with a posse of firemen
dragging their pumps and tubes

through the undergrowth

and shouting at each other
là-bas! là-bas!
in an effort to get to you
before you landed

and set another forest
on fire.

Fugue

Amazing, but a lark is treading air and singing
Beethoven's Fifth at six times Rattle's pace,
which someone has recorded and slowed down.

Yes, it's unmistakable: not just those first dramatic
chords (fate knocking at the door), but the cascade
of little notes that follows, bars of eggshell pizzicato,

crescendos to burst his chest, make feathers fly,
phrases plucked out of the sky like giddy moths
and sewn together in his beak – how wonderful

to chance upon a mad uplifting fact like this,
when I come home dog-tired, drained of music,
only fit to switch the TV on. And if a lark can sing

a symphony, what other melodies might fly,
if we record a sound and slow it down:
the Mozart in a busy road, the Elvis of a train?

who knows, an old man shouting on the bus today,
a mother crying for her son, may turn out to be
one of Bach's great fugues, so difficult to play.

On Hearing Joshua Bell Play Schubert's Fantasy in C Major
while my left leg is in cramp

No work of Schubert begins
more hauntingly than this: the rustle
of a piano tremolo, the violin
that seems to fly out of the trees
and hover in the air above our heads.
But just as time slows almost to a stop,
my left calf cramps:
I choke a cry, impossible to tell
if this is pain or just another music,
surely Joshua Bell has been injected
into my leg and is treating every muscle
as a string to bow or pluck,
so that I feel myself an instrument
in the making of his melody,
a violin listening to itself and shivering
with every note.
There is no way of knowing
how long a cramp lasts:
it is a masterpiece, a fantasy of pain,
and when it's over, I feel like clapping.

The Dog Who Thinks He's A Fish

It's on a plane that Harry tells me about his dog:
a pointer with the long ears and square muzzle,
the strong, spare body that locks into position
like a well-oiled gun when it's primed to shoot,
except that Harry's dog not only likes to swim
like a labrador fetching ducks, but like a fish,
that is with head immersed and eyes wide open
staring into the sea, coming up to Harry underwater
and shoving his nose up close, letting out a bark
that sounds like a small thud and sends ropes
of excited bubbles floating to the surface.
Never mind the legs thrashing and the tail trying
its best to wag and steer at the same time,
forget the lack of gills or of any attempt to sieve
a bodyweight of plankton through his teeth:
this is a dog who sees no difference between
himself and fish, enjoying the element of both
and a good shake between the two –
which isn't far removed from me and Harry
knocking back a drink and chattering like
small brown sparrows as our plane takes off.

She

She is a big woman who needs champagne
to help her celebrate or cry. So no surprise
to see a third bottle bobbing in the bucket,
as we sailed towards tears like a rocking canoe.
There was thunder and a storm of people
with seafood in their open mouths,
laughter cracking with the crab claws,
bruises of vinegar growing on linen.

A sudden urge to run from food, wine, her.
Christ, to escape before she poured her grief on me.
To hide in a dark room with just myself for company.
In my own time, I'll fall child-cut like Sky into the sea.
To cry in private, with or without tears, out or in.

But there was no getting away that night:
she started suddenly,
almost before the moment had arrived.
She didn't lift a hand or cloth to wipe away her tears.
She cried water clearer than vittel,
running down her cheeks and nose
                like condensation on a glass,
dripping on cockle shells and broken claws.
She washed her plate in tears
(I half expected her to dry it with her hair)
and people stared, but then so what?
She made the simple act of shedding tears
into an archetype, so clumsy, loud, and public
that the world looked round open-mouthed:
how Mother Earth wept for her child.

Looking back I recognize it as a skill.
The first time, she cried in a small way, trial run,

unused to giving tears their head.
I cried too, but did I know I was already dwarfed?
Slowly she learnt to build a diaphragm of breath,
to sluice the reservoirs of feeling, hurl her caution to the sky,
now anywhere she goes,
on crowded streets or cat-nap alleyways,
in well-raked parks or dainty shops,
she cries big as a rainforest, open as a can of worms.

I walk with her and try to be as big.
But there is a way in which a woman can be big for all of us.
We can shout with mouths full of fish.
We can break crabs, sluice wine and poison our tongues
with little spikes from the seabed.
But we had better leave the crying to a big woman.
She has the diaphragm to hold it. She can let rip
like thunder, draw down the electric bolt
and stand bang in the way when it strikes.
It is a job for big women. We should love them for it.

Coffin Cake

Next door's couple who were once
so sweet together that we winced,
are shouting at each other now,
hurling insults at the wall,
shaking the floor with angry feet;
while we have just crept back
from my nephew's birthday party,
speechless with sausages and jelly,
dizzy on loose-lipped dogs
and little cousins threatening
to jump into the pond like frogs,
the kitchen table dominated by
a thrilling castle of Victoria sponge
complete with its dastardly sheriff
and pools of jammy blood ...
but Johnny's favourite was still
the coffin cake his mother made
when he was five and mad on skeletons:
he'd not forget its liquorice lid,
the wine-gum handles, icing-cobweb,
and a long white hand reaching
out of the dark delicious box.

Just Because

i.m. Patrick Durrer

Just because he died doesn't mean
he's not here leading a normal life,
getting up late for breakfast and school,
bringing friends back for a sleepover
once a week, never tidying his room.

Just because the truck was going too fast
and he was too young to judge distance,
doesn't mean his mother can't sit quietly
and watch him playing soccer with his dad
or thumbing a gameboy in the back seat
when they drive to Tesco's.

And even though it happened years ago,
the impact grows like greasy hair.
He's seventeen now, five foot nine,
he plays the guitar and his eyes
are soulful as a labrador's.

Just because it's futile doesn't mean
they don't dream. They have a ghost
like other people have a pet.
And they have the charm of people
who are not quite of this world,
quiet as a couple of dog whistles.

Fishing with Elizabeth Bishop

For Isao

In a vast oatmeal valley
where clouds swim
over the brown loch
and shake off the water
like hunting dogs
when they reach the shore,

where a little white hotel
is rooted to the spot
like a dumb sheep,
the guests also sheepish
but determined to fish
until the last light,

in long green waders
and orange anoraks
fit for a battered oil-rig,
back-packed with tea
and lardy cake
and salty sandwiches,

with rods swaying
and the cork handles
snug as mice in our hands,
our pockets restless with
reels, weights, hooks,
clinking our Odin

and Abu Koster spoons,
an old tobacco tin
of lobworms, maggots,
tiny wriggling squats

for loose-feeding
the peat-black shallows –

we are approaching
the last day of our
fishing week,
time to steady
the jittery rowing boat
and push off onto the loch.

We have taken
Elizabeth Bishop with us
for luck and she sits
at the prow of the boat
with her delicate age-spotted
fingers combing the water,

as though she expects
a fish to see them as bait
and rise from the depths
of his home, knowing
how she will delight
in his appearance,

how she will notice
that his skin is infested
with white sea-lice, his lips
hung with fish-line
and hooks, like medals
with their ribbons.

She is not a ghost or
a poetic device, she is
not even a book of poems
wrapped in a plastic bag

and placed on the wet
wooden slat in front –

she is just the memory
of a poem, but there is
something very substantial
about her, fishy even,
so that neither of us
doubts her presence,

nor that having her
in our own rented boat
with the clouds
nosing around us
on the impenetrable water,
will eventually produce

a fish, who will surely
be as tremendous
and venerable as hers,
who we will observe closely
and possibly throw back,
or possibly decide to keep.

Willow

A bonsai willow sitting child-like
on the sill outside our bedroom,
is the first thing that I see
this morning as I wake up
dreaming of gigantic redwood trees.

Slowly my eyes focus
and the little willow becomes older,
more mature, though not much larger
in the process. I can trace the ruts
where copper wires once twined
round every branch, knots where
shoots have been removed and caulked.

This tree is so much smaller
than my dream. But it is an aberration
which makes the dream seem more realistic,
as if my whole today will be
a miniature of everything I dreamt,
each new leaf perfect as a bound foot,
mocking the scale of my imagination.

ODYSSEY

'Huckleberry came and went, at his own free will.'
(Mark Twain, *The Adventures of Tom Sawyer*)

Polyphemus

We were studying the Odyssey that day.
      At midnight, Polyphemus
(also known as Hairbrush or the One-Eyed Git)
      surprised us in the kitchen.
We offered him some smoky bacon crisps,
      but he slippered us instead.

Back in the dorm, I snuggled up with Twalt.
      In retrospect we thought
we'd been a little too compliant with authority,
      next time we'd have to douse
the lights and run, or plunge a red-hot poker
      into Polyphemus' eye.

I don't remember if we did get more heroic.
      Spetch would say,
It's bloody stupid having midnight feasts,
      but I enjoyed the plan
of copying the Odyssey, especially the bit where
      I escaped under a hairy ram.

Scylla at Whitby

I remember nothing about the Synod
or Captain Cook and his Whitby cats,
in fact it may have been Scarborough
that I dreaded going to for the day,
convinced the sea would be rough and cold
with Matron barking at us to change
into our puny swimming trunks,
as though she had six vicious curs
kennelled underneath her skirts.

But the day was sunny, the beach
a line of skinny see-through boys,
the sea so rough and playful
that it churned us into pebbles.
Matron took her shoes off, smoothed
her skirts and lavished us with towels,
chunks of bread and cheddar, lemonade:
so different, she made us all feel half
grown-up, but more than half still pups.

Sirens

For Spetch, it was the woman who sold sweets
and always called him 'Darling'
as she squashed her tits on a gob-stopper jar.

For Crone, it was Matron in her crisp white coat,
hand on his forehead, fingers on his pulse,
the lovely smell of lemon soap, her tree-trunk thighs.

Twalt would have dashed his ship for Mrs Stock,
that silky voice, the way her bottom rolled up to
the piano stool and then engulfed it in a wave.

But I preferred a magazine I'd nicked
from somewhere in the town, long afternoons
spent studying the glossy girls

in breathless detail, poring, fingering
each page as if to will it into skin,
and so amazed at this kaleidoscope of nipples

that Twalt said they'd have to tie me
to a bedstead, blindfold,
before I drowned them all in seas of spunk.

Lotus Eaters

If we hated all the food and the tapioca most,
because it was lumpy and grey in pond-size tureens,
for fear of newts and frogs lurking just beneath the skin,
sure they blistered the surface with slimy burps –
then why the rush for seconds, why craters filled
with strawberry jam, why look forward to Tuesday tea?

And if we hated it enough to lie in bed at night
saying *Spetch, are you awake? I'm hungry, Spetch.*
Why don't they give us something we can eat in this dump?
and someone, probably Twalt, would tell us to *Shut up*
and go to sleep, you lumps of lard – then why dream
of pudding ponds, red frogs leaping out of the jam?

If we hated it so much that any dollop on a plate
could win the prize for most resembling Spetch's spooge,
or fly across the room to decorate a portrait of the Queen
(the risk of hairbrush, ruler, blackboard duster, even
the comfy slipper) – then why, when we were sitting
in the dining room, did we never ever think of home?

Calypso's Island

Not till the last night, dangling our feet over the sill like a river bank, did Twalt call me a prat for leaving, and a toffee-nosed southern tosspot, but I agreed with him saying: I don't want to go, I just want to be in one place for long enough to call it home, even this sill will do if we stay perched here all night watching stars slide across the sky like shove-ha'pennies, or snuggle down in the back-seat of your dad's Rover licking frozen Mars Bars, then dive into a hay-stack in one of the fields and grope around like worms in an apple.

Don't know what you mean, says Twalt, who's only lived in one place, one small farm in a windy valley with cows and a dung-brown Rover in the barn, him scruffy blond as his mum's chickens, smooth-cheeked as the eggs she cracks on the rim of a pan and scrambles with butter, calling to us out of the cracked kitchen window – a boy who can't believe Nestles is Swiss, has never been south of Hull, thinks all good things come from Yorkshire, and school, well that's exciting just because it isn't home.

Ithaca

After stripping the bed at midnight and snuggling in with Twalt,
after stuffing crisps and an egg sandwich in my pocket
                   and running for the bus to York,
after sitting in a train for hours munching crisps and reading
                the *Eagle* very thoroughly,
after saying hello to my Universal Aunt and thank-you for the ice-cream
                  while we waited for my flight,
after choosing a window seat and holding my breath for take-off,
after visiting the cock-pit on my own,
after feeling sick and staying in the loo for a long time,
after combing my hair and trying to get my shoes back on
                 before we landed,
after walking down the steps with my shirt soaked in sweat,
after showing my passport and picking up my sky-blue Antler case,

I remember coming through the gates and seeing Mum and Dad,
and for a moment it was only the dog who knew me.

The Music of Fish

For the fourth day, no fish, not even a bite
and the gillie's cheery ways are starting to grate.
He says I'm the man who almost gave up
but on the last day landed a salmon so majestic
that it took two hours of guile to reel him in.

Only I'm still without the salmon.
And in this state I begin to think the worse of fishing,
I'd rather like to throw my rod into the water
and take up something else, perhaps a bagpipe or a flute
and sit there rocking gently on the loch
serenading the invisible fish who must lurk in its depths.

But I wonder what music a fish likes,
if water lapping a lazy boat could be his jazz,
if thunder, rain, a bagpipe all above the surface
can penetrate down to his ear and give him pleasure,
indeed if there are fish who croon or sing the blues
in their own liquid language? And if there are such fish,
might one be waiting for a flute accompanist, to sing
the song of his life, a sort of swan song of the deep?

Perhaps I shouldn't wait for a fish to bite,
but dive in myself, enter his world, follow my line
to the spinner and sit there in the green silence.
Until he arrives quietly out of the fog,
toothless, jutting-jawed, a blotchy exhausted kelt
who hangs transfixed before the lure
and shivers like a tuning fork.

Garden Square

A friend has borrowed my key.
I would like to enter and read a book,
but I do not want to wake him

or disturb the sunshine on his face,
as it looks like he's brought
his own spotlight into the garden

and I am witness to the act
of his amazing sleep, outdoors
in the middle of a great city.

It is the acclaim I can give him
not to shout for entry,
to leave my key snug in his pocket

and my hands not clapping
at my side, while the beasts of traffic
roar over my left shoulder.

My role is to prowl the fence,
to guard its heavy gates
from families with fractious babies,

to scowl at baggy teenagers
who want to kick a ball around
or float long-distance frisbees.

I will bend branches,
shunt the jutting roof of a house
out of the sun's path.

I will beat back the clouds
and my finger-tips will turn down
the volume of the afternoon.

The Weather at Work

*Never send a poet to London! The serious business of putting
a price on everything leaves nothing untainted.*
Heinrich Heine, *Travel Sketches 1826-31*

Today, a nimbostratus has followed me
into the underground,
where I'm strap-hanging with an anthology
including Pound and Frank O'Hara,
and everyone around me hunches their shoulders
as if my cloud might cause a storm.

It's certainly black enough, growling like a bear,
and bolts of lightning poke their nails out of its stomach.
But I'm not scared of rain:
I'm a petal on a wet black bough,
I'm Frank O'Hara on my way to lunch with
excitement-prone Kenneth Koch in Soho or St Germain,

or I'm a petal on its way to lunch
in a lovely sunlit poppy-field in Provence,
or maybe I'm a lunch of petals, a chef's own salad of poppies
growing dark and velvety between the tracks,
fed axle-grease manure and watered by a nimbostratus
as it follows me to work –

but when I get there, will there be hundreds of emails
cumulating in the sky, a blizzard of tricky faxes,
bargains crackling, hurricanes of futures purchases and sales?
Or will it be a calm day, all horizontal pens
and phone-banks drizzling as we discuss where to have lunch –

though to be honest, we always end up going
to Pizza Express on Victoria Street
or Simply Nico round the corner in Rochester Row,
because they're reasonably priced
and they know just how to peel a coat off at the door,
or leave you black with rain as you glower at the menu.

In Memory of Katoon Bekhor
        who loved this garden

There's a bench around the tree
    like an anklet, her name on it
        as if she were the tree's mother,

a frail leaf-handed woman,
    slightly gnarled in voice and skin,
        uprooted as a child, then replanted

here – how she must have loved
    to push aside this heavy gate
        and stroll along the flowerbeds

like streets where families of Spanish
    bluebell settled in the sixties,
        past a chatty dogwood from Quebec,

a sturdy Himalayan rhododendron,
    swathes of Chinese honeysuckle
        and the blazing Hokusai cherry tree

which throws off all its blossom
    in a week, as if embarrassed
        by its own extravagance.

She would have seen this city garden
    almost as a city in itself –
        a melting pot of languages

that plants speak through their skin,
    and which she understood
        or maybe not, but felt herself

always perfectly at home in the
    immigrant beauty of the garden,
        mothering every plant and tree.

Balzac's Granny

It started with the coffee-pot, or maybe
just before that at the moment when
my granny tripped and toppled head-first
down the steps into the House of Balzac.

She was revived with coffee, sitting
like a little rag-doll on the tapestry
of Balzac's chair, as pale as if she'd sat up
all night long to write her masterpiece.

Next door was Balzac's famous coffee-pot,
a white and purple porcelain sitting
primly on its matching warming tower,
just like my granny on a plumped-up cushion.

Against the silence of the coffee-pot,
her chatter percolated through the house
and made me think how fictionally
French she was: Balzac would have loved

to write her sitting at his desk,
recovering her fragile poise after the fall,
the Hermes scarf a little flustered
on her neck, a hair or two disturbed,

but her enthusiastic nose beginning
to enjoy the full aroma of the blend –
perhaps a plot-rich Bourbon/Mokha
like he used to brew himself.

And as the excitation of the coffee grew,
he might have stopped his scribble
for a moment, just to revel in the lovely
rolling r's which she produced.

Eggs

Even after a row, when bits of hurt
lie around the kitchen like unwashed plates,
you take three eggs in your hand
and break them cleanly on the edge of a bowl.

Each egg has two yolks and a small sack
of blood which breaks on contact,
but you do not flinch, you whisk through
the difficulty and add a dash more milk,

a twist of pepper, some chopped garlic
that you fry on its own at blistering speed,
and the omelette you make now
tastes even better, the outside is crisper,

the inside an even more delicious blend
of wet and firm, as if you are trying to show
that you are unaffected, that whatever happens,
you will still be able to cook perfect eggs.

Bread

The letter was all about bread.
And about a mother who was bread
in the way she rose like a loaf
and fed everyone around her,
in the heat of her body when she slept
and the yeasty texture of her skin.
She was freckled as a sesame roll.
She could be thin as toast
or thick as a slab of soda bread.
She had the trick of being fresh each day
and big enough to break
and share with the whole family.

The letter, in calling her bread,
made her really feel like bread.
There was no butter in it,
to call it a bread-and-butter letter.
No thanks for any particular gift
or best wishes for a special date.
It was just about bread, the sort
that people buy or bake each day
and eat without much thought.

This is Helen's most amazing letter,
she said, and put it in the bread bin
to keep fresh.

Her Arm

Three days we sit and wait for her last breath.
Her arm rises out of the coma and hangs
like a bat in the eaves, silent, hearing things

beyond us. There are photos spread over the bed:
mangoes bursting out of their skins, a small white dog
clutched in her arm, a carpet coughing on the washing line,

and by the Cuzco road a huge turquoise butterfly
just beyond the reach of her net. I can see it
writhing in a jam-jar on the back window of the car.

We know her arm so well, each freckle is the marking
of a butterfly, how the skin feels soft and thick
as bread when she's had a bath. But none of us

can summon up the courage to touch it now,
or bring it back to earth. I think that when it drops,
that movement will herald her last breath.

For if anything about her, any limb needs rest,
it is this arm. And if she lifts it now, it must be doing
something only arms can do, not hanging

like a bat in the eaves or spying on our sorrow,
but picking one last mango from a tree, let's say,
or placing a small flat stone in her burial wall.

ETHIOPIA

Lemon for love, lemon for love,
lemon you smell so sweet, lemon you are so tasty.
(Ethiopian song)

NOTES

Wot and injera is the national dish of Ethiopia. *Wot* is a spicy stew and *injera* is the fermented bread that you use to scoop it up. My father hated it, especially the business of eating with his hands. This was a source of much laughter in the family.

No one imagined the terrible wars and famines, which were to come much later, after Haile Selassie was deposed.

During Lent, traditional cooks like **Asfaw** would stick to a vegetarian diet and sometimes make 'fish' or 'eggs' out of chick-pea flour.

Harar, an old emirate city in the east of the country (where Arthur Rimbaud once lived and traded) is famous for its **Hyena** men. They sit along the outskirts at night and feed packs of wild hyenas with meat hanging from their mouths. Hyenas are often associated with sorcery and witchcraft.

Lalibela is a small town in the north, famous for its magnificent rock churches. The story goes that a prince was attacked in his cot by a swarm of bees. Miraculously, they did not sting him and his mother called him *Lalibela,* meaning 'the bees recognize his sovereignty'. When he became king, he built the famous churches, to thank God for his survival. They were finished very quickly, because angels carried on the work at night.

Timkat is the Ethiopian Coptic feast of Epiphany, the commemoration of Christ's baptism. In legend, the Queen of Sheba's son by King Solomon, Emperor Menelik, brought back the Ark of the Covenant to Axum in the north of Ethiopia. Now all churches in the country have a replica Ark which is paraded down to a pool for the baptism ceremony. The priests are decked out in splendidly embroidered robes and parasols.

Map

Adigrat, Adwa, Axum,
Makale and Gondar,
Inticho, Debre Tabor, Lalibela,
Debre Markos, Dessie
and Addis Ababa,
Nazaret,
south to Lake Langano,
east to Awash and the train that skirts the Ahmar Mountains
snaking down to Dire Dawa,
south again like Rimbaud's caravan
past hyenas at the walls of Harar,
to camels on the plateau of the Ogaden,
to Kebri Dehar, Warder, Geladi,
Kibre Mengist,
Kelafo,
Dolo.

Double Exposure

A hall in Addis Ababa, summer
1964, and Geraldine is dancing.

Back then, I was scared of her legs,
and this photo's got four of them,
shooting out of her blue tutu
like bolts of lightning from a clear sky.

It's as if she's only earthed
by her points, so fierce and graceful
is the charge running through both
of her twelve-year old bodies.

Her career was over in an afternoon
like a summer storm, but Dad was always
proud of his shot: *best one I ever took,*
he'd say, *look, look, she's moving.*

Praise Poem for Asfaw, the Best Cook in Africa

His belly has the roundness of cooking pots.
His smile is always generous to boys.

His teeth are yellow like home-made beer.
His fingers are chunks of stew.

He lives in the steam from kettles.
His breath is a lemon tree.

His hair is a thorn-bush.
He can use it to scour the frying pans.

When he laughs, he is making beef sausages.
When he sighs, it is a fasting fish.

His yard is full of important chickens.
He has knives for every neck.

Dogs love him for his gristly bones.
Sheep trot up to him and bleat.

He is the father of Abebe and many other sons.
He is the husband of Aster.

He cooks all day to feed his families.
He is a hundred wooden spoons.

Missing Africa

What did he miss, now he was sentimental?
Could it be the reek of eucalyptus trees,
the wot and injera that drove him mental
by slipping through his fingers, all those fleas,
mosquitoes, tsetse flies, hyenas, ants,
explosive nose-bleeds from the altitude?

He had a gift for complicated rants,
but sometimes like a sunny interlude,
he could wax lyrical at lunch about
a wattled starling, or he'd call for Asfaw
in a booming voice to say his mutton stew
was simply heaven (praise the Lord for stout),
while Asfaw beamed up to his beetle brow
and served the coffee, with a sprig of rue.

Black Madonna

I know she didn't have a pair
of blue-winged angels or a haloed son.
It wasn't red and gold she used to wear
when dusting in the dining room,
but with her soft black skin, her scarf,
she looked a lot like Mary. Every day
she cleaned the wooden frame and laughed
when mother said 'Aster, that's twice today.'

One Sunday morning, no-one else awake
but me, and I was in a trance,
I saw her walk up to the picture, take
a breath and disappear. The only sound
was parchment rustling at the glass.
Then Mary seemed to spot some dust and frowned.

A Lament for the Ostrich

My mother, you had eyes like nesting eggs,
you were generous with the warmth of your feathers,
you ran bolt upright and your neck swayed like the stem of a rose.

One day you built a stable out of packing cases,
you put children on a donkey, you named a puppy Daisy,
you spoke to many people and told them what to do in a nice way.

At the market, bananas jumped into your shopping bag,
grapes ripened in your hand, prices tumbled like apples from trees,
you gathered new friends like a warm wind picks up leaves.

At noon, the car of your husband returned along a bumpy road,
you welcomed him with whisky and soda, you stroked his cheek
and let him rest after lunch with his head on a cool pillow.

In the evening, you brushed your feathers, kohled your eyes,
put perfume on your warm skin, everyone who saw you
wanted to touch your skin and smell the lacquer in your hair.

My mother, I am your two-toed son.
When I think of you, I am running bolt upright,
my neck is a rose stem swaying and my eyes float like eggs.

Hyenas

Outside the city walls, at night, there was a man
    who came out with a bag of meat
    and sang, under his breath, a list of little names.

He put a chunk between his teeth and waited
    for an oily chuckle from the shadows,
    then the first hyena, gingery, black-spotted,
    would slip into the light and sidle close
    and tug a strip of gristle from his mouth.

There was something almost of a kiss in it,
    the meat like lips just asking to be
    chewed – no leg or arm stuck out for balance,
    just two black noses nearly touching,
    two thick necks joined at their gleaming teeth,
    and a pencil line of muscle as they strained
    to pull apart, but slowly, with restraint,
    perhaps even a growled reluctance.

And each hyena slipping from the pack
    ignored the bag of meat,
    to feed at the man's mouth.

Malaria

Ice-cold, I cry out in the night.
A light comes on over my bed
and nurses zero in like moths.

They eat away my soaking sheets,
my blue pyjamas, dab my body
with their furry arms, their wings.

I shut my eyes and lips but still
they crawl into my ear, as if
there is another light inside my head:

my brain's a ward for animals,
and in the corner is a donkey
suffering from malaria, like me,

except his sweat smells of fresh hay
and when he is in pain he spreads
his lips and brays like a baby.

The King of Lalibela

At night, the angels help me dig.
They come on warm currents
over the mountains like migrating moths,
their wings drenched with sweat,
arms like brickies', three-day stubble.

They break rocks with their bare hands,
sometimes water bursts into
their smiling faces, glistens their afro hair.
Thick red clay flies out of the bore,
as if they were unearthing a bone.

A flat-roofed church appears, tall
as a saint. An angel with a wasp waist
squeezes through the tiny window,
he carves me an altar stone, paints the walls
in a trice with sticky frescoes

of St George lancing the fiery dragon
from his prancing horse, while opposite,
a blue Madonna cups the baby Jesus
on her lap. I have a mother
who reads to me and holds me when I'm hot,

but I'm still scared of nurses, bees, syringes,
anything sharp and full of liquid.
I wear a hammer in my belt, a chisel, brushes.
There's plenty of sweat but no shiver,
when I cut stones with the angels.

A Daughter and Two Diseases

The woman in the next bed
has a daughter and two diseases:
malaria, like me, and elephantiasis.
Her huge distorted legs lie
beached and bloated on the sheets,
as if they'd been fished out of a lake.
When a fever comes, she shakes
the bed, rattles it on the pipes
until the whole room is ringing.
The skin round her ankles is thick
and pebbled – sometimes it opens
as if cut with a knife from the inside,
and puss bubbles out of the cracks.
Nurses rush to dab and dress her.
She looks at me apologetically,
says something in Amharic, moans.
Her hands are long and delicate,
soft as ostrich feathers – sometimes
she spreads her fingers in a veil
and covers her face as she cries.
In the afternoon her daughter comes,
when the light is starting to fade.
She speaks gently and holds
one of her mother's beautiful hands.

Timkat

Still now, I half believe it would have
fallen off, if I'd not stopped right there
and made a vow to find religion –
conveniently the night before Timkat,
when we all got up at five to watch
a hundred deacons of the Coptic church
arrive out of the morning mist
like beetles glittering in candlelight,
encrusted in their robes and parasols
that bristled like antennae in the breeze,
and now the little dapper Emperor
(dressed head to toe in mothy beige)
stepped lightly from his car
and chatted with a grizzled Patriarch.

Somewhere in the throng, an Ark
was swaying on its way to the baptismal pool,
but Dad's dawn photo captured just
this boyish deacon, twitchy as a dragonfly,
and me, by contrast sickly pale,
a little gothic creature of the night,
left eye as fishy as the mirror of a Flemish master,
holding the tiny white reflection of a smile.

Wheeler-Dealer

What do you do? people ask me at parties,
so I tell them straight I'm a wheeler-dealer,

not that I deal in wheels, but my deals
have many spokes, they take the toughest hills,

the steepest valleys in their stride,
and sometimes they turn so fast I feel blood

whistle in my veins and my nimble bottom
chafing on its poky posture-pedic saddle,

I grip two phones like handlebars and race
towards the line, a ticker-tape reception

of me madly waving my arms and shouting
like I've just invented the wheel –

and not that bumpy Fred Flintstone type of wheel,
but a sleek ferocious mesh of metal rods,

with the tiniest strip of rubber burning the asphalt,
like a plaster torn off a scratched knee,

like the word YES written in smoking sulphur
in the middle of a perfect circle,

like Leonardo's perfect man stretched
to the limits of his circle, and still turning.

Neck

The nudity of it is delicious and cool,
like an iced pear sitting on a plate.

Alone in this room of ruffs and collars,
it is saying how good it feels to be a neck,

to have the same number of vertebrae
as a giraffe, the same grace as a swan,

and since it looks like a delicious fruit,
it invites appetite, a slight salivation

in the viewer's mouth, or else
as happens in my case, a sudden urge

to kiss its nape, as though it is a photo
of my lover rather than the portrait

of Sir Thomas Wyatt, painted just a year
before he lost his head and therefore

made this neck, still perfect in its
flexibility and in the carrying of blood,

superfluous, a limb that might as well
be clothed or not exist at all.

Except, it is so beautifully painted
that even with no head attached,

it might continue to draw eyes
and make the odd lip quiver.

He

He was like wire in a rubber coat.
I thought at first he might be frayed and spark
a fire in my hands, but he did not.
He flexed, fumed, hissed and spat like fresh-cut bark
thrown on the fire.
                              He glowed like fakir's coal
from underneath his skin. He flinched from touch
and singed my fingers when I tried to hold
him close. His eyes like fists could send a punch
exploding in my face.
                              In self-defence
or fearing love, he plays the hurricane
and scalds the freshest garden with a breath.

But when I dream, I see his mud-red feet
that fire the tinder fields of sugar cane,
and blind the sky with smoke, pitch black but sweet.

Totem

When you go away, even for a week,
I like to rebuild you from scratch.
I approach it slowly, like making a face
from a skull or the body of a caveman
from his footprints in the ash.
I use what's to hand, a toothbrush,
a nail clipping off the carpet,
creams that line the window sill,
a few black hairs from the bath
which I plant in a pot like cress.
For skin, there's a chickpea recipe
from Claudia Roden's Jewish cookbook,
your eyes are purple olives from a tin
we keep just for emergencies,
and yes, your heart's the travel clock
which you wound up, then forgot to pack,
dashing out to the mini-cab with a frantic wave
that I imagined was a signal to all
remnants and reminders of you in the flat,
to club together and keep me company.

The Sadness of Dogs

Because I never see him,
I will never know his breed or colouring,
the length and floppiness of his ears,
the way his tail might wag or slip between his legs in fear,

but it's enough to catch the rattle of his chain
and hear him howling
from the next door garden over the whine of traffic
and the terrible shrieks of mating cats,
to picture how he is inside and want to join him
in the expression of his loneliness.

We have that much in common
for this is a night devoid of other dogs or boys to play with,
and I feel that somehow I should let him know we're sharing
the loneliness, as if it were a drinking bowl.

But no-one has taught me how to howl,
neither the range and subtleties of a wolf, nor yet
the simple messages of dogs who may be dreaming of the pack
and catch a sniff of having once been wild.

Camel

Like a camel, I can go for miles without a drop of poetry.
In the morning, sweat flowers from my armpits
and my feet trudge steadily through office dunes,
but by five my tongue is threatening to snake out of my lips
and head for a waterhole.

As soon as I get home, I dip into the bookcase
and take a swig of Walcott, letting the sand on my tongue
dissolve, tasting the sea and the rum, nosing
through the islands where words can make you feel
like shipwreck and rescue in one hit.

Perhaps it is dangerous to be so moved, courting
the risk of an attack of Lawrence or a gush of Donne
in the middle of a meeting. One phrase, like water bursting
from a cactus, conjures up imaginary pools,
and makes the desert seem much drier than it did before.

Who but Robin?

Who but Robin would have six novels sitting
in his underpants drawer, six novels as sharp
as Jane Austen with a knife in her hand,
as broad-shouldered as Tolstoy riding
through the snow in a padded Cossack jacket?

Who but Robin would turn up to lunch
with the publisher, without a single page
to show for all the guilty hours of writing,
and then get drunk on vodka tonic within
the first ten minutes of their sitting down?

No-one but Robin would have said
with total innocence that he writes like
himself, and then when pressed again,
when told that everyone writes like someone,
pick Jane Austen and of course Tolstoy:

*I write like a mixture of Jane Austen
and Tolstoy.* I can hear him say it,
with another gulp of vodka tonic,
squinting squarely at the publisher,
daring him to wrench open that drawer,
to push aside the underpants and take
the novels out, if only he were man enough.

Crusoe's Brain

This is my brain on holiday – it's June,
Bird Island – there's the little runway where
we landed on the left, the golden rim
of coves and beaches where we lie all day
and never see a soul – just birds high up
that wheel and grow into a thunder cloud
as dark and choppy as the sea – and there
right in the middle is the restaurant
with woods on either side, the tables laid
with fish and fruit, a waiter serving drinks.

My brain looks happy on its holiday,
the pickled walnut shape has lost its edge,
when doctors touch my head I feel my brain
relaxing into every crevice of the skull
as though it's shucking off its canvas shoes
and going for a walk along the beach –
my love, I see it turning red as snapper,
I hear it humming to itself like birds
released into the sky and dizzy from
the sunshine beating on their feather-heads.

My brain is thinking that it would be nice
to stay here on sabbatical, a book
of poems in its hand, and call itself
Crusoe or Man Friday, and go fishing
for snapper in the afternoon or meet
up with your brain for an ice-cold beer,
no messages to read or send, no nerves
to calm or complex thoughts to organise –
my brain might never make it back to me,
just send a postcard wishing I was here.

Little Pieces of Common Life

i. Lunch

I keep a postcard of Chardin's lunch
on my desk while I munch a sandwich.
It's so simple, just a cup of red wine
and a tempting slice of cured ham.
Perhaps someone is coming with glittery
oysters and lemon wedges, rosy apples
or bunches of fat grapes for afters,
but all he has now is ham on a pewter plate,
wine from a green bottle that's so discreet
it's fading into the background, not even
the silver cup can manage more than
a calm reflection of his dog-nosed fork.
But that doesn't stop me rushing to
finish my sandwich, so that I can ease
this beautiful bone-handled knife
out of the ham, and carve myself a slice.

ii. Pot

Because I love the warm brown skin
of Chardin's coffee pot, the way
its awkward handle juts out of the body
and the lip is small, pursed, almost shy
of hot liquids, I pick up a stoneware jug
and work my fingers over its homely glaze,
the rim of little chips and roughnesses,
foot bare but for a number 6 or 9.
And I think how much I'd like to have
the hand of a warm elderly woman to touch

when I'm looking at a photo of my Mum,
not as a necessity, not that looking
doesn't conjure up the feel of her already,
but purely for pleasure, a little tactile luxury.

iii. Bubble

Not to the second son of the apple-peeler
or the pot-scourer, the turnip-scraper,
not even to the brat of the scullery-maid
or the kitchen girl whose job it was
to polish silver, endlessly – but to
this boy sitting underneath the barrel
of a laundress with her hands bloated
by the soapy water, her wide eyes
looking out of the picture as if Chardin
had suddenly called out 'Cheese! ' –
to him, at the end of his straw, the bubble
has emerged and grown fat, glistening
like fish, and his eyes so fixed on it
that they appear closed from this angle,
a mimic of pursed lips, cheeks stopped
with a pocket of air, his chubby fingers
clamped to the wet umbilical straw –
he could be the son of his own bubble,
just a breath away from bursting.

Still Life with Niece and Skull

As for man, his days are grass. (Psalm 103)

Do we need an armadillo shell, a wormy peach?
Or is it plain enough, just sitting here together
on a hillside covered with arthritic trees
and geriatric grass, outcrops of shale that simply
crumble under our boots? True, the dog's found
a sheep skull and well and truly buried her nose
in the eye sockets, the loch down there is wrinkly,
full of spots that may be otters or old age,
and your fingers chart the edges of my bald patch
like a headstone – but I'm still a bit surprised
to hear you say: *Uncle, do you miss your youth?*

Well, I may be guilty of warm mittens
and a fleece, my feet feel nicely socked and smug
just nesting in their new expensive boots,
I'm savouring the prospect of unbottled
heaven in my glass of Oban whisky, relishing
the deep-sea flavour of the fresh crab
your dad is promising to dress for us tonight,
and how your button nose will wrinkle in disgust
at it's not being pasta and cheese,
how your eyes will sparkle in the firelight
as we sit around telling Japanese ghost stories.
But no, Katie, I don't miss my youth. I have yours.

The Cabinet of Curiosities

From the diary of the French consul, Alexandria, 1831

A letter has arrived today
from the Head of Customs in Marseille:

he's starting a collection
with the mummies of a woman,

a lizard and a cat, so he'd like
an ox or a giraffe, a spiky

five-foot snake or morsels of old bread.
He's heard about a baby with two heads

which would fit nicely with the jars
of malformed foetuses

and vulture-entrails in formaldehyde,
that are a source of pride

to show off to his visitors
or study with a friend behind closed doors.

I think I'll write and offer him the joy
a fourteen-year-old boy

whose viscera have been
removed, wrapped up in resinated linen

and replaced,
mud slipped beneath his face

to stop the contours of his skin
from falling in.

And when the boat arrives,
I bet the Head of Customs' eyes

will bulge out of his head,
at such a young example of the dead.

The King of Scythia

Towards the end, he bought gold,
worked it into decorations for the reins,
hammered out a golden bit and coated
the blinkers with a film of gold leaf.

Every last penny he spent on it,
the gas allowance, ciggie money,
hocked an old watch that didn't work,
cashed in the last premium bonds.

When he was ready, he dug a large hole
at the bottom of the garden, put on
his best clothes and went to the stable.
I'm going to ride to Heaven, he said.

What To Do With Clothes

When I go, let me have nothing
that I don't need with me.
Let me be like the old man
who went hopping down the road
on a Saturday morning, with his
clothes dropping off one by one,
so that when he got to the beach,
he only had his large black shoes,
and those he untied very slowly
while humming a tune, now
he had all the time in the world.
Or if I must still have clothes,
let them be useful, like a coat
with big pockets that I can weigh
down with stones, if I ever need
to finish things off like
Virginia Woolf in the River Ouse.
I'll spend the next few years
trying to offload the things
I spent my life acquiring.
And those I have left, let them be
like snake skin getting tauter,
more transparent over time,
so that I'm left naked in the
middle of my clothes, my things,
and have no trouble stepping
out of them, when it's time to go.